For Geoff and Gina.

I hope these little rhymes
bring you happy smiley times.

Best wishes

Cathie Nevile.

16/9/97.

THE MARVELLOUS MENAGERIE

Caroline Nevile

MINERVA PRESS
LONDON
MONTREUX LOS ANGELES SYDNEY

THE MARVELLOUS MENAGERIE

ISBN 1 86106 377 6

First Published 1997 by
MINERVA PRESS
195 Knightsbridge,
London SW7 1RE.

Printed in Great Britain
B.W.D. Ltd, Northolt, Middlesex

THE MARVELLOUS MENAGERIE

For Eta, Alex, Ann,
Cliff and Chris.

Contents

The Bimbly Bumble Bee

"Hello, it's the bimbly bumble bee!
Have you come to talk to me?"
He looked but didn't reply
Seemed more interested in the sky
Small and round, yellow and black
Where did you get the lovely mac?
Suddenly he grew much madder
He puffed himself up like an adder.
"How dare you say such a thing?
You deserve a nasty sting!"
We parted company
Bimbly bumble bee and me.

Scurrie the Squirrel

Scurrie the squirrel was always very busy:
Just to watch him made me dizzy!

He'd rush around the garden at a hundred
miles an hour
Never pausing to see a pretty flower

He had one thing on his mind
To hide his food from animal kind

But alas the place he chose
Was just beneath my favourite rose

And now in the place where it should be
A sycamore stares back at me.

The Acrobatic Cat

Cyril was a silly cat
Who thought he was an acrobat.
He tried again and again
Swinging from the climbing frame
With this in mind and fully primed
He set off at a run
Looking for some fun
At last the frame came in sight
He leapt with all his might
But alas in mid-air
To poor Cyril's despair
He nose-dived in a spin
His legs crossed under him
He landed in a crumpled heap.
So much for his flying leap!
Cyril was no acrobat
Just an ordinary cat.

The Tiger

There's a tiger sitting on my lawn
All tattered and torn.
I told Sarah Lee,
"Invite him in for tea,"
But what if he eats me?

hopper 47

The Kangaroo

If you see a kangaroo sitting on a bus,
don't stop and stare and make a fuss.
He's probably tired of hopping
whilst doing his shopping.

The Wiggly Waggly Worm

Hello, its the wiggly waggly worm
He makes some people squirm.
He wiggles and waggles on his tum
Clinging to the ground like chewing gum
He hasn't any knees you see:
If he had, he'd walk like you and me.

The Elephant

Why do you suppose
an elephant has a long nose?
Is it to clean his toes?

The Happy Hippo

I saw a hippo trying to climb a ladder
And nothing could be sadder.
Every time he raised a great big foot
The ladder broke, kaput.
Instead of climbing through the air
He fell below to his despair.
He sat on his enormous bum
And felt absolutely glum.
If the ladder was as strong as he
What a happy hippo he would be.

The Happy Elephant

I saw an elephant in Safeway's store
and followed to see what he was looking for.
He paused in the second aisle
and gave a happy smile.
He reached up for a sticky bun
and it disappeared inside his tum.
"Please Mr Elephant, for that you must pay!"
He shook his head in a sad sort of way.
"I'm very sorry, it's my first time shopping all alone
and I'm afraid I've left my purse at home."

The Slug

The short fat slug
Is an ugly bug
But to his mum and dad
He's a handsome lad.

The Slimy Snail

Hello, it's the slimy slithery snail
His head is so like his tail
How can he unravel
Which way to travel?

40

The Snail

The slimy slithery snail
Stumbling slowly along his trail
Carrying his home wherever he goes
Pausing often, his journey's slow
His home if it was plastic
Would make his speed fantastic.

The Curtailed Cat

If a cat had three legs
Instead of four,
Would he miss his other paw?
Would he think it nice
To frighten little mice,
To hit and throw them in the air?
I bet he wouldn't dare!

Mr Fox

Hello, it's unconventional, undercover Mr Fox,
And just look at those socks!
His tail is up, his head is down, he's on the run:
Mr Fox is looking for some fun.
But wait: he stops awhile
And gives a foxy smile.
What's this he's found upon the ground?
Is it hidden treasure?
He sniffs it for good measure
He raises his head and gives a call
To summon his friends one and all
Swiftly, silently, like Concorde
They arrive to applaud
What Mr Fox has found upon the ground:

A golden ball,
Quickly they form a ring
To examine the thing,
Soon a game is in full swing,
They laugh and shout and fool about
And pass the ball between one and all
But all too soon
With the fading moon
They have to leave their game
And head home down the lane.
Every fox, young and old
Remembers what they've been told:
"slink away before the sun appears
Or man will put a bullet through your ears."

The Crafty Cat

The mirtly mistle thrush
Disguised himself as a holly bush,
But for him, unfortunately,
The cat was disguised as a chimberly.
Now no one for the mistle thrush mourns:
His song is heard whenever the cat yawns.

The Rat

Jack was a naughty lad
who enjoyed being bad;
He broke every teacher's rule
when he took his rat to school.
He put it in his pocket
and just forgot it
until his teacher bent to check a sum
and it bit her on the bum.
She cried out in alarm
and it bit her on the arm.
Jack knew he was in trouble
when he was marched to the Head at the double.
"Well boy, what is it this time?
What is your heinous crime?"
Poor Jack looked so humble
he could only mumble,
"Please sir, I brought my rat to school."
"What, you silly little fool,
I'll phone your parents at once:

you're nothing but a stupid dunce."
A tear fell from Jack's eye
and he began to cry.
"Please sir, don't, I'll get the cane.
I promise I won't be bad again.
I'll be as good as gold
and do as I am told."
The Head stared at him in consternation
and rung his hands in frustration.
"How can I trust you
after what you put your teacher through?"
Jack hung his head in shame
and promised to be good again.
"My boy you need a kick in the pants
but I'll give you one more chance."
Jack looked at the Head in disbelief
and smiled with relief.
And to this day he has never broken any rule
and I've heard he even enjoys going to school!

The Magpie

Do you think the magpie knows he's a bird?
I ask because his walk is so absurd.
He doesn't hop like most birds do;
He struts like an adjutant in blue.
His great big legs pound the earth
much to the little worm's mirth.
He holds his haughty head up high
and nothing escapes his beady eye.
But to catch a worm he hasn't a clue
he just doesn't know what to do.
So instead of eating them for his dinner
He starts to strut and looks much thinner.

The Ladybird

Have you ever seen a ladybird cry?
Until yesterday neither had I.
She sat on a bright green leaf
breaking her heart with grief.
Her scarlet coat
was as wet as a moat.
I asked her why she was so sad,
surely nothing could be that bad.
She replied in a whisper
She had lost her little sister.
Her mum and dad would be hopping mad.
It wasn't the first time you see
She had also lost the other three!